FORMATIVE
ASSESSMENT

FORMATIVE ASSESSMENT

{ Shirley Clarke }

CORWIN

SAGE Publications Ltd
1 Oliver's Yard
55 City Road
London EC1Y 1SP

CORWIN
A SAGE company
2455 Teller Road
Thousand Oaks, California 91320
(0800)233-9936
www.corwin.com

SAGE Publications India Pvt Ltd
B 1/I 1 Mohan Cooperative Industrial Area
Mathura Road
New Delhi 110 044

SAGE Publications Asia-Pacific Pte Ltd
3 Church Street
#10-04 Samsung Hub
Singapore 049483

Editor: Delayna Spencer
Senior assistant editor: Catriona McMullen
Production editor: Nicola Carrier
Copyeditor: Sharon Cawood
Proofreader: Emily Ayers
Indexer: Adam Pozner
Marketing manager: Dilhara Attygalle
Cover design: Naomi Robinson
Typeset by: C&M Digitals (P) Ltd, Chennai, India
Printed in the UK

Library of Congress Control Number: 2020938050

British Library Cataloguing in Publication data

A catalogue record for this book is available from the British Library

ISBN 978-1-5297-2655-8

At SAGE we take sustainability seriously. Most of our products are printed in the UK using responsibly sourced papers and boards. When we print overseas we ensure sustainable papers are used as measured by the PREPS grading system. We undertake an annual audit to monitor our sustainability.

This book is dedicated to all the wonderful teachers around the world who tirelessly inspire and encourage our children to reach ever higher goals, but especially all the teachers from my learning teams over the last 20 years. The ideas in this book are evidence based but originated from them. Thank you for keeping formative assessment alive and ever-evolving.

TABLE OF CONTENTS

{ ABOUT THIS BOOK }

Bridging the gap between research and practice, *A Little Guide for Teachers: Formative Assessment* gives teachers practical tried and tested strategies to put formative assessment into action in their classrooms.

- Authored by an expert in the field
- Easy to dip in-and-out of
- Interactive activities encourage you to write into the book and make it your own
- Fun engaging illustrations throughout
- Read in an afternoon or take as long as you like with it!

Find out more at
www.sagepub.co.uk/littleguides

{ ABOUT THE SERIES }

A LITTLE GUIDE FOR TEACHERS series is little in size but big on all the support and inspiration you need to navigate your day-to-day life as a teacher.

- ⊕ CASE STUDY
- ▯ HINTS & TIPS
- ◇ REFLECTION
- ▧ RESOURCES
- ▤ NOTE THIS DOWN

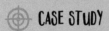

ABOUT THE AUTHOR

Shirley Clarke is a world expert in formative assessment, specialising in the practical application of its principles. Many thousands of teachers have worked with Shirley or read her books and, through them, the practice of formative assessment is continually evolving, developing and helping to transform students' achievements.

Shirley's latest publications are *Visible Learning Feedback* with John Hattie (Routledge, 2019), *Thinking Classrooms* with Katherine Muncaster (Rising Stars, 2019) and several On-Your-Feet Guides, published in 2019 by Corwin. Her website (www.shirleyclarke-education.org) contains a videostreaming platform of clips of formative assessment in action, as well as detailed feedback from her teacher learning teams.

Shirley can be followed on Twitter on:

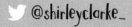 @shirleyclarke_

INTRODUCTION

Formative assessment is a set of teaching and learning processes that empower children not only to progress but also to become owners of their learning. Summative assessment is the measuring or testing of learning so far and is quite different in its design. Formative assessment is all about good teaching and learning and enabling progress rather than measuring it.

Think of formative assessment as the following elements, all of which overlap and depend upon each other to maximise their effectiveness:

- setting the scene to create confident learners
- organising effective talk and discussion
- establishing learning intentions and success criteria so that children know the purpose of their learning and how to reach the goals
- uncovering children's understanding through questioning and on-the-move feedback
- helping children know how to identify success and understand how to improve.

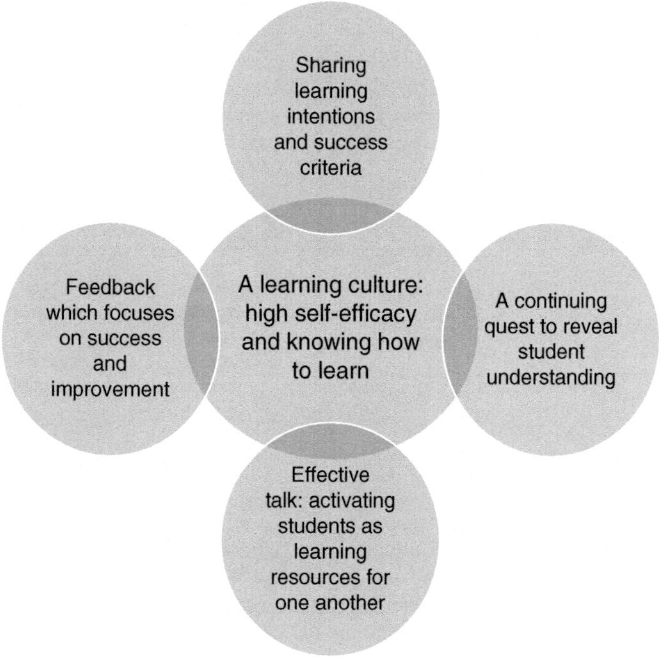

Figure 0.1   Elements of formative assessment

This book will take you through these elements, giving key research evidence and tried-and-tested classroom strategies.

CHAPTER 1
SETTING THE SCENE –
HOW DO YOU CREATE
CONFIDENT LEARNERS?

This chapter looks at ways of creating a culture for effective formative assessment. Topics covered include:

- Developing self-efficacy (belief in our ability to achieve)
- Knowing about the brain and learning (cognitive science shows the limitations of our working memory)
- A language of learning (knowing what learning consists of).

DEVELOPING SELF-EFFICACY

There are many barriers to self-efficacy, all of which stop children believing they can achieve their very best. These are (a) believing that the teacher has a low opinion of them and their ability; (b) being worried about making mistakes; (c) reward systems which compare children; and (d) being 'labelled' through being in an ability group.

It doesn't have to be like this! The following are some tried-and-tested strategies to give all children an equal chance at achievement:

- Love your children and be careful with what you praise and how you say it:

  - Make sure you show all the children you teach that you have their best interests at heart. Avoid subtle body language or tone-of-voice clues to children that you maybe don't like them or rate them (sighing, showing impatience at individuals, comparing children, etc.) – once they believe you don't value them, they stop investing effort in learning and might even disconnect from it.

  - Praise should be **task related** not **ego related** ('*You have worked hard on this and have two excellent similes*', not '*You're so clever! I knew you'd be good at similes.*') Ego-related praise reinforces that the child has little control over their learning and that the teacher's approval is paramount. It can lead to learned helplessness when a child is faced with failure, thinking that they are no longer clever.

'*Most praise is given to teacher perceived lower achievers, whereas most critical feedback is given to higher achievers.*'
Meyer et al. 1986: 293–308

o   Use the same tone of voice with all children when looking at their work, regardless of their achievement level. Give feedback about successes and improvement possibilities in their learning, regardless of their perceived 'ability level'.

o   Children are aware of excitable praise being given to lower achievers and more critical feedback given to higher achievers, and believe the difference relates to your high or low expectations of them – creating a self-fulfilling prophecy.

•   Normalise error!

'Errors invite opportunity. They should not be seen as embarrassments, signs of failure or something to be avoided. They are exciting, because they indicate a tension between what we now know and what we could know: they are signs of opportunities to learn and they are to be embraced.'
Hattie, 2012

o   When a child is stuck, don't sympathise – instead say 'That feeling of it being difficult is your brain growing' or 'You are about to learn something new!'

o   Tell children about the importance of mistakes because they mean you are on the brink of new learning. Tell them how scientists fail all the time until they get to the right solution, learning each time how to improve.

o   Show them the difference between a careless mistake, which they can usually self-correct, and a misconception, which needs more input from a teacher or another child.

o   Tell them that when you find something tricky, more neurons are connecting in your brain than when you find something easy! Finding something easy means you usually already know it.

o   When a child makes a mistake which is common to others in the class, place the work under the visualiser (or document camera) to project it and talk about the 'marvellous mistake', asking what has gone wrong and talking through the error and the solution. End by getting the class to say thank you to the child for helping us learn from our mistakes.

o   Display a poster of 'things to do when you are stuck' (see Figure 1.1).

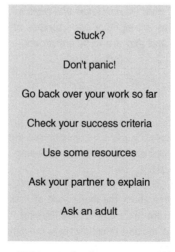

Figure 1.1   Poster of 'Things to do when you are stuck'

PUNISHED BY REWARDS!

Many successful countries do not give rewards for learning or behaviour, but see learning as the reward in itself. Lepper and Hodell (1989), among others, found that external rewards have a detrimental effect on intrinsic motivation. Children who don't get a reward are not motivated to work harder – not receiving one simply reinforces that whatever they did was not good enough. Rewards can never be fair, regardless of the criteria used, and make children either complacent or demoralised. This effect is invisible to teachers, because children rarely complain about the systems we put in place.

 IDEAS FOR THE CLASSROOM

- Ask children what they think about the various rewards in school and whether they think they are fair. Ask them how they feel when they don't get one.

- Explain that we will be celebrating everyone's achievements verbally, all the time – focusing on their successes and ways to improve (see 'On-the-move feedback' in Chapter 4).

- If you want to keep 'Child of the week' (common in primary schools), make sure every child in the class knows they will be chosen at some time to talk about what they are most proud of that week.

- Instead of rewarding individual children in assemblies, focus on skill or knowledge of the week, in which a whole class explains how they learnt a new skill or piece of knowledge, with first steps, success criteria, problems they faced and examples of their successes.

THE TROUBLE WITH ABILITY GROUPING

Placing children in ability groups sets expectations about whether a child is seen by the school as a winner or a loser. The child, in turn, believes this to be true and behaves according to those expectations, creating a self-fulfilling prophecy. Note that 88% of children placed in ability groups at the age of 4 are still in them by the time they leave school.

Children can be engaged in different levels of work, while sitting in a mixed-ability group, so it is not the learning which causes the problem, but the grouping, with its clear label.

It is illegal to group by ability in Finland, a consistently high-achieving country, before the age of 15. PISA studies (OECD, 2010) show that the more countries group by ability, the lower the student performance overall. (See Chapter 2 on the organisation of random learning partners, which creates instant mixed ability.)

'500 studies on ability grouping resulted in minimal impact on achievement but profound negative impact on student efficacy.'
Hattie, 2009

 ## IDEAS FOR THE CLASSROOM

- **For mathematics teaching, use either a mastery scheme (e.g. Singapore Maths) or tasks which are 'low floor high ceiling' (e.g. how many different shapes can you draw which have an area of 24 square centimetres?), which extend all children.**

- **In secondary school, try mixing Years 7, 8 and 9, with all maths teachers planning together.**

- **We should be activating children as learning resources for each other to maximise their learning. If pairs change** weekly or every few lessons, children get a chance to be both the explainer and the learner, according to the person they are randomly paired with each time. Often, children can explain things in a better way than teachers, especially if they are trained in how to be a good learning coach. Langford School in Hammersmith and Fulham developed such prompts for mathematics and English (see Figure 1.2).

Prompts for being a good learning coach in English	Prompts for being a good learning coach in mathematics
• Is there anything you feel you need help with? • What impact on the reader do you want to achieve? • Do you think you are achieving this? • How successful do you think you have you been against the success criteria? • How can you include this aspect of the success criteria? • You could use a simile/ metaphor etc. here. Can we think of one? • Can you think of a better word instead of ____? • Could you think of any adverbs to put before any verbs in your writing? • Could you ask the reader a question in your writing?	• Have you followed the success criteria? • Can you demonstrate that this is the right answer? Explain how you know. • Would a whiteboard help you? • Could you draw a diagram? • What is the rule for e.g. rounding numbers? • How do you know this number is e.g. divisible by 2/ prime/a factor of 32? • Let's talk through an example and go through the steps. • Ask me questions and interrupt me if you don't understand. • Now, can you do this example on your own? Talk me through it.

Figure 1.2 Useful prompts for being a good learning coach

Source: Langford School in Hammersmith and Fulham

KNOWING ABOUT THE BRAIN

We know that the more you are challenged, and the more you learn, the more neurons are connected, so you really can 'grow your intelligence'. Cognitive science has also illuminated facts about memory and how we learn best. The working memory (what we are thinking about and focusing on at any moment in time) is limited in its capacity to remember without props. Try transferring an 11-digit reference number from one place to another – we can only remember about 7 or 8 individual items at once! To give children any chance of remembering their learning, they need to be thinking about what we want them to learn, as we can only remember anything we have consciously thought about.

'Memory is the residue of thought.'
Willingham, 2009: 54

 IDEAS FOR THE CLASSROOM

- **Show children YouTube clips of neurons connecting (e.g. Neurons and What They Do – An Animated Guide by cosmiccontinuum at www.youtube.com/watch?v=vyNkAuX29OU) – it looks like outer space!**

- **Explain that our brains have endless capacity for learning and memory, and for growing our intelligence, with the following conditions:**

    Practice   Effort   Time   Input

- **Make a PETI poster and ask children to use this language when they are reflecting on their learning or are stuck. It is much more empowering for a child to ask for more input than to ask for help, for instance.**

- Display a bullseye diagram with three different coloured circle zones, labelling them from outside to inside: panic zone, learning zone and comfort zone. This will help to remind children that they should be in the challenge zone to be learning, unless they are practising something over and over and can move it to the comfort zone (e.g. times tables or formulae).

- Ease the cognitive load of children's working memories by:

    o   encouraging them to take notes

    o   providing copies of key facts, skills, and so on, for frequent reference, or displaying these on working walls

    o   labelling diagrams rather than providing a key

    o   modelling new skills in silence at the front, then asking a child to explain what you did (talking and modelling at the same time overwhelms working memory)

    o   making sure the correct focus is on what you want students to think about (have the exploding volcano at the end of the lesson, not at the beginning!)

    o   having frequent low-stakes quizzes and tests so that they are constantly retrieving things from their long-term memories and therefore making them easier to recall, by deepening neural pathways.

A LANGUAGE OF LEARNING (METACOGNITION)

Children can take more control over their learning if they know what learning actually is and therefore how to learn. Once children and teachers know how learning breaks down, they have a common language with which to talk about learning.

The Education Endowment Fund (EEF, 2018) found that, on average, using metacognition added the equivalent of an extra eight months of schooling to children's performance.

> 'Metacognition is self-evaluation, in which students are perceptive and honest observers and critics of their own performance.'
> Guy Claxton, 2018

IDEAS FOR THE CLASSROOM

- Introduce the learning powers in Figure 1.3, derived from the research of Claxton, Costa, Quigley and Clarke, one at a time. Link them with a character that embodies the characteristics. In primary school, this could be animals (e.g. tortoise for resilience) or superheroes; in secondary school, children can identify famous people or film characters. Focus in on one of the elements of each power. Say, for instance, that in every lesson today (or this week in secondary) we'll be looking at how well you can manage distractions.

- Refer to the learning powers in real learning contexts. For instance, discuss:

  - not giving up during some tricky mathematics or being cooperative during a partner discussion

  - learning intentions as well as asking children which learning power (and which element of that) they think they most need for the lesson. Encourage children to reflect on how well they used these powers in the lesson

o **which things help children learn (movers) and which get in the way (blockers). Students' responses will help you see how to help them learn best and will give a clear message that they are being listened to.**

Figure 1.3 Learning powers, derived from the research of Claxton (2002), Costa (2008), Quigley and Clarke (2010)

Table 1.1 shows the outcomes of a movers and blockers brainstorm with children at one school. Try it with your class – it can lead to a contract being drawn up between the class and the teacher.

Table 1.1   'Movers and blockers' brainstorming with children

MOVERS (help us learn)	BLOCKERS (stop us learning)
Having a learning partner	Too much noise in the classroom
Being able to see the whiteboard	Disruptive children
Liking the teacher	People talking to you when you're trying to concentrate
Being given enough time	
Getting advice about how to improve	Not enough time
	Losing stuff
Good behaviour	Not understanding the work
Having the right stuff (pencils etc.)	Feeling stupid
Understanding what to do	

Source: Nuthatch Primary School, Appledore

NOTE IT DOWN

DECIDE WHICH OF THE ELEMENTS OUTLINED IN THIS CHAPTER ARE WORKING WELL IN YOUR CLASS/SCHOOL, WHICH NEED SOME MINOR MODIFICATION AND WHICH NEED MORE CAREFUL INVESTIGATION AND THOUGHT. REMEMBER THAT TAKING THINGS SLOWLY AND DOING THEM WELL WILL BE MORE EFFECTIVE THAN TRYING TO INTRODUCE TOO MUCH AT ONCE.

Element of formative assessment	Working well	Need to modify	Need to start (add by when)	Need to investigate/ think about
Making sure children know I have their best interests at heart				
Only giving task-related praise or feedback rather than ego related				
Giving all children success and improvement feedback in the same tone of voice				
Celebrating error as an opportunity to learn				
Teaching about the capacity of the brain				
Having a 'What to do when you're stuck' poster displayed				

(Continued)

Element of formative assessment	Working well	Need to modify	Need to start (add by when)	Need to investigate/ think about
Eliminating comparative reward systems or giving all children the reward				
Having mixed-ability seating				
Focusing on practice, effort, time and input as the conditions and language for learning				
Using the learning zones bullseye poster				
Adapting teaching to ease the cognitive load				
Asking children what helps them learn and what stops them learning				
Introducing the learning powers/ including them in lessons				
Brainstorming movers and blockers				

CHAPTER 2
SETTING UP EFFECTIVE TALK - HOW DO YOU ACTIVATE CHILDREN AS LEARNING RESOURCES FOR EACH OTHER?

This chapter looks at setting up effective talk between partners and in groups, exploring the following:

- Rationale for random talk and learning partners
- How to organise random partners
- Ways to ensure quality of talk and equity between pairs
- Strategies for effective group work.

WHY RANDOM TALK PARTNERS?

Classroom discussion is high in John Hattie's list of influences on learning, with an effect size of 0.82 (.4 is the average effect size). Although 'turn and talk to the person next to you' is a popular strategy after a whole-class question is asked, as it gives children more 'wait time', my work with learning teams over 20 years has revealed that randomly chosen talk partners, changing frequently, lead to significant gains both cognitively and socially. It avoids children being stuck with the same partner for long periods and missing out on learning opportunities. Teachers say that having random learning partners changing weekly in primary and every five or six lessons in secondary, leads to:

- Instant mixed ability

- Better behaviour

- Higher quality written work (because the discussions act as rehearsals for writing)

- Inclusion (because 'hands up' is eliminated)

- Developing mutual respect regardless of gender, race, etc.

- Making new friends, so there are fewer cliques

- Great support for those with English as a second language

- More confidence in talking in front of the class

- Learning from each other, through discussion and through peer support

- Greater focus and better listening.

HOW TO ORGANISE RANDOM TALK PARTNERS AND ENSURE QUALITY

1.   Choose a way to pick random pairs: use an online randomiser, named lolly sticks in a pot drawn out in twos, or, for younger children, small laminated photos of each child drawn out of a bag in pairs and then displayed for the week.

'Peer tutoring has many academic and social benefits for both those tutoring and those being tutored. The overall effect of the use of peers as co-teachers of themselves and others is, overall, quite powerful.'
Hattie, 2009, citing, among others, Cook, Scruggs, Mastropieri and Casto, 1985

2.   Explain to the children the rationale that this will help them learn better, make new friends and give them a chance to learn from each other over the course of the year.

3.   Begin on a Monday morning with the random choosing. Children then sit in their pairs where you decide they should sit (they change seats every time).

4.   Co-create whole-class success criteria, to be displayed, for good partner talk. A popular strategy for co-creation is to role-play at the front, with another adult or a child, a partner discussion in which you do everything wrong (not holding eye contact, interrupting, etc.) and the other person is the perfect talk partner. Seeing the opposite approach makes it clear to children what good partner talk should and shouldn't be, and you can then brainstorm with them the success criteria for learning partners.

5.   Introduce end-of-week compliment slips for primary children (*Thank you for being my learning partner. I really enjoyed learning with you because…*) and self- and peer evaluation slips for secondary children, focusing on the success criteria and deciding where they need to improve.

6.   Ask for hands up only if someone wants to ask a question.

7.   After giving the class a question to discuss, say how long they have for this (not too long – e.g. 30 seconds), then pick a named lolly stick at random and ask that child: *What did you and your partner think?* It is more productive to ask for one thing to be discussed for a short time than to give a longer

time to discuss a number of items (e.g. *Find one strategy the author has used to add suspense to this writing and decide why it is effective. One minute – go!*). You then randomly choose children to give their ideas.

TYPICAL QUOTES

4-year-old: I like it when I sit with my talk partner because I listen better and don't fidget.

8-year-old: When we do something with a learning partner, it is good because you get double the ideas and your work is doubly better!

11-year-old: I think it is good that we can cooperate with anyone, then people don't just want to work with their best friend all the time and you can work with people you might not normally work with.

14-year-old: Talk partners work well because you share ideas and compromise. You understand things better.

Teacher: The children are more tolerant of each other; the language they use has shifted and it seems as if we are on the same team. There is less of a hierarchy in the class and everyone's ideas are valid, not just the high achievers. Children seem to have realised they are more equal and they are willing to work with anyone.

'An important strategy is when children become teachers of others and learn from peers, as this involves high levels of regulation, monitoring, anticipation and listening to their impact on the learner.'
Hattie and Donoghue, 2016

HINTS & TIPS

1. Make sure parents know in advance the rationale for changing partners to avoid confusion.

2. Remember that children should change their seat each week, unless they are on the autism spectrum or have a physical reason to stay in the same spot.

3. To ensure all children talk and listen, frequently change from 'Bethan, what did you and your partner think?' to 'Bethan, what did your partner say?'

4. By the third change of partners, this system will have become the norm and you will find that children are excited to change partners.

5. Don't be tempted to fix the pairings – one of the most powerful aspects of random pairing is how often unexpected pairings are successful. Two very quiet children together now have to learn to speak; two chatty children together now have to learn to listen, and even the two most disruptive children, paired for a week, are, apparently, better behaved given this chance than if they had been 'placed' by the teacher.

6. Because of the nature of random choosing, one child can end up with the same person too many times. In a class of about 30, throw the names back in the hat if two children have been partnered three times already. If a pair comes up two weeks in succession, also throw them back for that week.

(Continued)

7. **Try making threes occasionally, especially when one child has a language issue or is extremely disruptive.**

8. **Experiment with rearranging tables in the classroom. Teachers say rows or U shapes are more effective than tables of six, because all comfortably face the front and are less distracted by other children. Teachers can also then talk with individuals face to face rather than to the top of their head!**

TAKE IT FURTHER BY

- Spending more time on the meaning of the success criteria, giving examples and looking for excellence in the classroom. Take photographs of good or bad 'child paired talk' to discuss with the class: 'What does this show?'

- Introducing more sophisticated elements into the success criteria with older children, such as considering when to compromise and when to stand your ground, persuasion and letting go of what you want to say to listen instead.

- Extending the talk partner criteria by linking them with learning dispositions, such as resilience, cooperation, concentration, persistence and challenge seeking (see Chapter 1 for more detail).

- Developing self- and peer evaluation at the end of the pairing. This can be oral exchange with young children and more written comments from older children.

- Giving every child a question mark card (of playing card size) which they can place on their table above their work at any time they are stuck – this is an invitation for any child who sees it to leave their seat and spend a few minutes explaining to or coaching the child.

EXAMPLES OF CO-CONSTRUCTED TALK/LEARNING PARTNER SUCCESS CRITERIA THROUGH THE PHASES

Table 2.1   Strategies for effective group work

How to be a great talk partner	Our learning partner success criteria	Ground rules for learning partners
• Sit close together and face each other	• Listen to my partner's advice and use it in my learning	• Hold eye contact
• Speak clearly – don't cover your mouth	• Take shared responsibility for our learning	• Convey your voice
• Look at your partner when they speak	• Take turns and don't interrupt	• Listen; don't talk over each other
• Speak slowly	• Help my partner by offering suggestions	• Disagree politely
• Listen to your partner	• Understand that my partner might not agree with me	• Keep an open mind
• Don't interrupt	• Share my ideas with my partner	• Use persuasive arguments to express your opinion
	• Hearing is waiting for a gap so you can speak; listening is being able to let go of what you want to say and instead listening to what is being said	• Encourage each other
		• Share responsibility for learning
		• Respect each other
		• Develop your communication
		• Inspire each other
		• Don't give answers; guide instead

STRATEGIES FOR EFFECTIVE GROUP WORK

If organised well, group work can have many benefits. The four-year 'Spring Project' on paired and group work (Baines, Blatchford and Kutnick, 2017) found that:

- It raised levels of attainment and deeper conceptual understanding and inferential thinking.

- Student behaviour improved as children took more personal responsibility.

- Group work doubled sustained, active engagement in learning and more than doubled the amount of high-level, thoughtful discussion.

- Teachers' professional skills and confidence were enhanced and their teaching repertoire extended.

First of all, the task needs to lend itself to group discussion and shared responsibility, with clear goals and success criteria; then the group needs to be organised to ensure that all have equal say and equal input. To make tasks challenging, and motivating yet achievable, they need to have an end goal but one in which the means to get there is not obvious or has many possible routes to success *(e.g. How many shapes can you draw with an area of 24 sq. cm?)*. Some might even have no right or wrong answers, but require ideas to be pooled and debated (e.g. *Decide the qualities of a true friend/Decide how best to spend $1000 to improve your school, giving justifications*). Closed tasks, on the other hand, with one right answer (e.g. *Find the area of this circle*), are unsuitable for group discussion, as clearly either the problem could be solved by either all children individually or, as part of a group, the child with the quickest right answer will be the only one doing the thinking.

Success criteria co-constructed with children for what it means to be a good group member, provide a constant reference both for teachers and children. Siciliano (1999) determined the criteria for 'an ideal team member' as being four deceptively simple elements. These can be used as a starting point which the class could then add their ideas to (see Table 2.2).

Table 2.2   The criteria for 'an ideal team member'

Do your part	Complete the tasks assigned to you
	Be willing to put in the time necessary to complete your team assignment
	Ask if there is anything you can do
	Pull your own weight and do your share of the assignment
Share your ideas	Express your opinions
	Respond to other group members' ideas
Work towards agreement	Be open to other ideas, opinions and perspectives
	Be willing to work together
	Work as a team (not just on an individual basis)
Keep a positive attitude	Maintain a sense of humour
	Be courteous
	Give feedback in the form of constructive criticism

Source: Siciliano (1999)

Effective organisation strategies for group work are: (a) snowballing, (b) assigned roles, and (c) Jigsaw:

a.   *Snowballing* is the term often used to describe an activity where children first discuss in pairs, then join another pair and share their thoughts. This can then continue up to groups of eight, all sharing their ideas. This strategy works very well when ideas need to be pooled to get the best of all ideas. It also works well when there are different ways to solve a maths problem, for instance.

b.   *Assigned roles*, such as manager, recorder, reporter, questioner, ensure that all children contribute equally. These roles need to be described first and young children can be given a badge to wear during the task, showing their role. Over different tasks, the children experience the different roles. Assigning roles lends itself best to discussion or debate, such as 'Should animals be kept in zoos?' or 'Is the brain better than a computer?'

c.   The *Jigsaw* strategy is highly effective when a body of knowledge needs to be taught and understood in the best and most efficient way, and is most suitable for upper juniors or secondary children. Here's an example:

Imagine a task where we have five readings based on the Ancient Greeks (Olympics, art, scientists, gods, philosophers).

1.   The children sit at tables of about 3–5, and agree who is A, B, C, D and E.

2.   Person A on each table reads and makes notes on one of the elements (e.g. Olympics); Bs do the same for art; Cs on scientists, Ds on gods and Es on philosophers. All have about 12 minutes.

3.   All the As then meet together, similarly the Bs, Cs, Ds and Es, to talk about the main messages (about 15–20 minutes).

4.   The children then return to their original groups and report back the major findings and understanding to the others.

5.   Each group shares its major ideas and a whole-class discussion is held to ensure that all understand the main themes underlying these five practices.

NOTE IT DOWN

DECIDE WHICH OF THE ELEMENTS OUTLINED IN THIS CHAPTER ARE WORKING WELL IN YOUR CLASS/SCHOOL, WHICH NEED SOME MINOR MODIFICATION AND WHICH NEED MORE CAREFUL INVESTIGATION AND THOUGHT. REMEMBER THAT TAKING THINGS SLOWLY AND DOING THEM WELL WILL BE MORE EFFECTIVE THAN TRYING TO INTRODUCE TOO MUCH AT ONCE.

Element of formative assessment: random learning partners/ group work	Working well	Need to modify	Need to start (add by when)	Need to investigate/ think about
Sharing rationale with children and parents				
Choosing a random selection process				
Co-constructing learning partner success criteria				
Introducing compliment slips or evaluation cards				
Beginning the process of random partners				

(Continued)

Element of formative assessment: random learning partners/ group work	Working well	Need to modify	Need to start (add by when)	Need to investigate/ think about
Eliminating hands up unless using named lolly sticks to pick who answers a question				
Linking success criteria with learning dispositions				
Trialling rows or U-shape seating				
Trialling the question mark card				
Experimenting with snowballing pairs once random pairs are up and running				
Assigning roles in groups of four for discussion tasks				
Trialling the Jigsaw strategy				
Co-constructing success criteria for being an effective group member				

CHAPTER 3
LEARNING INTENTIONS AND SUCCESS CRITERIA – HOW DO YOU CLARIFY GOALS AND BREAK THEM DOWN?

In this chapter, you will learn about:

- Knowledge and skills; open and closed skills; and decontextualised skills
- Co-constructing success criteria
- Everlasting success criteria
- Writing up learning intentions and success criteria.

KNOWLEDGE AND SKILLS

The curriculum is all knowledge; even those things we call skills are, in effect, procedural knowledge. That said, I continue to differentiate between skills and knowledge because they are usually taught differently. Knowledge is factual and skills are procedural, with learning intentions that look like those in Table 3.1.

Table 3.1 Learning intentions for knowledge and skills

To know properties of 2D shapes (knowledge)	Decide whether these are **skill** (procedural) or **knowledge** (factual):
To know the key events of the Second World War (knowledge)	• Times table facts
	• Writing a characterisation
	• The impact of steam power
To be able to write a letter (skill)	• Solving quadratic equations
	• Using watercolours
To be able to solve quadratic equations (skill)	• Properties of 2D shapes
	• Multiplying with the column method
	• Key events of the Great Fire of London
	(Answers can be found at the end of the chapter!)

We usually link knowledge with skills like this:

To know key facts about The Great Fire of London (knowledge) linked with –

To write a newspaper article (skill).

Knowledge is either taught or researched, with knowledge organisers commonly given to students to aid recall and to provide a reference to key facts during the learning.

Skills are most helpful when broken down into the steps or ingredients, commonly known as success criteria. Knowledge breaks down into facts rather than process steps or ingredients. Success criteria, therefore, are most helpful when teaching skills.

SKILLS: OPEN (TOOLS) AND CLOSED (RULES)

Success criteria (effect size .77) break down the skill learning intention into specific elements and help students know *how to achieve the learning intention*. They are most helpful if they give the process steps or ingredients needed. Closed skills, such as grammar and punctuation (e.g. to use reported speech), and many mathematical procedures, have compulsory ingredients (rules), whereas open skills (e.g. to write a characterisation) have a menu or toolkit of possible inclusions (tools), as in the further examples in Figure 3.1.

Rules skill (compulsory ingredients): once mastered the LI is achieved	Toolkit skill (menu of possibilities): success criteria don't guarantee quality; they give suggestions of what could be included
L.I. To find half of a number (Year 1)	L.I. To write a story opening (Year 4)
Remember to: 1. Check you have the right number of counters: 2. Share them out into two groups, one at a time. 3. Count how many there are in one group. 4. Check both groups have the same number.	**Choose all or some:** • Setting: dialogue, description, end at beginning • Hook the reader: show not tell, suggest what might happen or have happened • Use senses • Create powerful images for the reader • Use our 'what makes good writing' success list

Figure 3.1   Examples of rules and toolkit skills

CLOSED SKILLS LEAD TO MASTERY

Once children have learnt a closed skill (e.g. how to multiply two digits by two digits), achieving all the compulsory success criteria, they have achieved mastery and there is nothing else to learn about that skill. There is no quality continuum: attainment for everyone who has mastered a closed skill is the same, albeit some might be quicker at it than others.

OPEN SKILLS KEEP DEVELOPING

By comparison, open skills (e.g. a characterisation and most writing), in which children have a menu of possible inclusions as success criteria, are skills which they learn to improve for the rest of their lives! Ask any author if they have achieved mastery of their writing and they would probably say they are continually learning. This means that, although a child might have used the success criteria options, their inclusion doesn't guarantee quality. There needs to be, alongside the success criteria, classroom analysis of excellent examples so that children develop an understanding of 'what a good one looks like'.

MATHEMATICS SUCCESS CRITERIA (THREE TYPES)

Success criteria need to reflect the learning intention, so for (a) a specific maths procedure, for example, there would be **clear compulsory steps (remember to…)**; for (b) a more open learning intention of, for instance, multiplying given numbers (once this has been thoroughly explored), the success criteria might give **a choice of different methods (choose from…)**. When students are given (c) word problems to solve (e.g. how many minutes have you been alive?), the most helpful success criteria would be **problem-solving criteria,** such as estimating first and drawing diagrams to help you.

DECONTEXTUALISED SKILLS

Many skills can be transferred to different contexts, as shown in Figure 3.2.

Instead of telling students they are learning to design a poster for, for instance, the Christmas fair, first discuss what makes an effective poster, co-constructing the success criteria. Once these are generated, they can be used every time that skill comes up, regardless of the context.

Figure 3.2   Skills transfer, using the example of poster design

Obviously, when the effective poster criteria are used, students also need knowledge pointers for the linking context, otherwise you could end up with all the success criteria for a poster fulfilled, but with inadequate content. Perhaps there could be two columns on the whiteboard/flip chart – one for the skill success criteria and one for today's knowledge content (see Figure 3.3).

There are many other skill learning intentions like this, that are important to first discuss in their decontextualised form, so that the success criteria can be transferred to any context. Here are some examples:

- To be able to write an explanation text

- To write instructions

- To write a formal letter

- To solve maths problems

- To use information retrieval
- To write a balanced argument
- To design a fair test
- To create a characterisation.

L.I. To design an effective poster (transferable skill)	For today's lesson: a holiday in Paris
Remember to include:	Think about:
• All key information • An easy-to-read font • Good contrasts • An eye-catching design • A main message in the biggest lettering • Pictures, if useful, which emphasise the message	• Sightseeing highlights (e.g. the Eiffel Tower) • Examples of accommodation • Excursions • Travel possibilities (e.g. the Metro) • Food and drink • Culture (museums, history, theatre, opera, etc.)

Figure 3.3 Skill success criteria and knowledge content

CO-CONSTRUCTING SUCCESS CRITERIA: SIX KEY STRATEGIES

'The Closing the Gap Construct
The learner needs to:
Possess a concept of the goal
Compare the actual level of performance with the goal
Engage in some appropriate action which leads to
some closure of the gap.'
Royce Sadler, 1989: 119–44

Sadler's famous construct of how to 'close the gap' emphasises that, first, the learner must 'possess a concept' of the goal. It doesn't say 'know the goal', but 'possess a concept of the goal', which can be achieved by not only knowing the learning intention, but also understanding how it breaks down into criteria which help the learner achieve the goal. Co-constructing success criteria by analysis of excellent examples or comparing good and poor examples as a common strategy, makes the concept of the goal even clearer. Once students know the goal, the success criteria and what excellence does and does not look like, they are in full possession of the goal. Without all of these, it would be like being given instructions to make a chocolate cake with no recipe, instructions or picture of how it should look; or to try to build a table with no clear goal (size, material, style?), criteria for success or a chance to look at good and poor examples and what makes the difference.

Whether open, closed or decontextualised, success criteria have maximum impact on children's learning if they are co-constructed. Not only do the students internalise and more easily remember the criteria, they also have a greater understanding of their meaning. The following are the five best, most time-efficient and worthwhile strategies for co-constructing success criteria, with examples.

STRATEGY 1: GIVEN 2-3 EXAMPLES, 'WHAT FEATURES DO YOU SEE HERE WHICH MAKE THESE EXAMPLES EXCELLENT?'

With writing examples, it is better to have short extracts rather than long pieces. To co-construct criteria for suspense writing, for instance, I might write two short texts on the whiteboard:

Mia stood in the dark and listened. She could hear something breathing...

The huge car park was empty. Not a soul was in sight. Julia's car was the only one left. As she walked towards it, she could see something or somebody standing beside it...

The reason for more than one example is to make sure children don't copy the style of the text we analysed but can see different versions of excellence. This is particularly important in writing.

Read the first sentence, then ask the children to talk to their talk partner for 30 seconds to identify one technique the author has used to create suspense. Take their responses, writing up the ideas as you go. Make sure you only take elements which are specific to suspense, rather than those features which would be appropriate for any writing. The success criteria for both examples could be as follows:

- The main character is alone.

- The setting is threatening (with darkness, fog, a derelict house, woods, a remote place, etc.).

- The threat is unnamed (somebody, something).

- The verb chosen (breathing) suggests something scary.

- There is use of an ellipsis.

- The sentences are short.

 HINTS & TIPS

1. Children might need you to start them off if they can only see features such as 'short sentences'. An effective strategy is to say, for the first two criteria: 'Does it say "Mia *and all her friends* stood in the dark and listened"?' They will quickly see that being alone gives it more suspense.

2. Similarly for the other criteria, we could ask, 'Does it say "Mia stood in the *brilliant sunshine* and listened"?'; 'Does it say "She could *hear her baby daughter breathing*"?'; 'Does it say that she could hear something *chirping*?' and 'Does the sentence end with *an exclamation mark?*'

3. By comparing the non-threatening version with the original sentence, the children can understand and appreciate the techniques the author has used.

STRATEGY 2: COMPARING A GOOD EXAMPLE WITH A BAD EXAMPLE

The juxtaposition of excellent next to poor is powerful in making clear what is and is not good. Seeing what makes an effective poster, for example, would be clear to children if they are shown a professional printed poster next to a poor poster, in which there is missing information, unclear fonts, non-contrasting colours, all the same size writing and no eye-catching images. Keep children's work from previous years and you will have access to anonymous excellent and poor examples which become a great resource for co-constructing success criteria.

Instead of asking young children to draw a self-portrait by looking into a mirror (it is very difficult to transfer 3D to 2D), present them with a self-portrait done by a talented teaching assistant or a teacher next to a self-portrait that you have drawn, deliberately making it awful – no eyebrows or neck, the wrong colour hair, and so on, which will make them laugh but again also makes it clear what should be included by viewing the juxtaposition of the two self-portraits.

This strategy can be used effectively for many learning intentions, such as:

- Any punctuation skills versus sentences not punctuated:

'Help!' cried the girl, ' I'm all tangled up!'	Help cried the girl I'm all tangled up

- Any grammar skills versus incorrect grammar:

We came home and saw a kangaroo in the garden!	We come home and see a kangaroo in the garden!

- A balanced argument versus a biased argument
- A correctly set-out line graph versus uneven axes and incorrect plotting

- A correct sentence in French versus an incorrect sentence in French

- Clear instructions for making something versus very unclear instructions.

  And so on!

STRATEGY 3: DEMONSTRATING AT THE VISUALISER/ DOCUMENT CAMERA

A visualiser is an essential classroom tool, as with it you can project anything instantly onto the screen. One effective use is to demonstrate how to do something, using the visualiser, stopping at each point and asking 'What did I do first?', 'What did I do next?', taking the children's responses and writing up the criteria as you go. Use this strategy for any skill which has different ingredients or techniques, as in the following examples:

- Demonstrating how to use a particular art tool (e.g. inks or water-colours), where you keep stopping to gather the criteria about how to hold the brush, how to mix colours, how much of the medium to use at a time, etc.

- Demonstrating how to look up some information for an information-retrieval learning intention (where to start, use of indexes, or internet searches and what to do)

- Demonstrating how to use a dictionary

- Demonstrating how to draw a line graph.

STRATEGY 4: DEMONSTRATING HOW NOT TO DO SOMETHING AT THE VISUALISER/DOCUMENT CAMERA OR BY PERFORMING AT THE FRONT!

When you think children have a little knowledge about something, playing at not being able to do something correctly sends them into calling out what you're doing wrong and what you should be doing instead. Obviously, this would be inappropriate for a skill which children have had no experience of, so it works well to consolidate previous learning and is fun to use with young children. An example of the possible contexts you could use is to demonstrate with 4- and 5-year-olds how not to count properly (over-counting first until they tell you how to organise the cubes so that you can count them more easily; then not moving as you count so that you still don't know which ones you've counted; then going back to the beginning again rather than stopping at the last one). You should end up with the following criteria, with helpful pictures beside them, through correction by the class:

- Put them in a line
- Count every single cube
- Move each one as you count
- The last one in the line is the total in the group.

The following are also suitable for demonstrating how not to do something, with children correcting you at each step. They have to phrase the success criteria so that it makes sense, so this strategy is very useful for developing language fluency:

- How to put on a coat
- How to form letters
- How to use scissors correctly
- How to tidy up the role-play area.

STRATEGY 5: FINDING THE MISTAKE (GOOD FOR MATHS CALCULATIONS OR ANY PROCEDURE WHICH HAS DEFINITE CHRONOLOGICAL STEPS)

Children love to find mistakes, given an example with an error. You can make up something yourself or use an anonymous example of a maths calculation from a child's work from a previous year. Look at the example in Figure 3.4 and try to spot the mistake.

> **Spot the mistake!**
>
> 18×5?
>
> $10 \times 5 = 50$ $8 \times 5 = 45$
>
> $50 + 45 = 95$
>
> $18 \times 5 = 95$

Figure 3.4 A 'spot the mistake' example

You will have noticed that you have to start from the beginning and check every step to check for accuracy. This means that you can ask children, after they've found the mistake (8 x 5), what you do first, what next, and so on, writing these up as you go, on a whiteboard or flip chart or, better still, a Perspex-covered display board, written straight on as a reference for the next few days or for as long as they need it.

STRATEGY 6: EAVESDROPPING

When the learning intention of the lesson is something which you believe the children will probably already know quite a lot about, simply ask them to talk to their learning partner for a minute or two, to list all the ingredients or steps. In the meantime, walk around the room jotting down what you hear, revealing the list to them (written up on display) after the time is up. If they have missed out any elements, don't be worried about adding your own ideas – it is co-constructing after all.

Examples of learning intentions suitable for eavesdropping are the following:

- To write a newspaper article
- To write an invitation
- To write instructions
- To write an informal letter.

For older children, this strategy can be used for learning intentions which you know they will have covered in previous years.

Even with this quick strategy, however, we need to remember that analysing what a good one looks like, and often a poor example too, takes children's understanding to a higher level. So, after gathering the ingredients of an invitation, for instance, the next step would be to *look at two examples of invitations, one with missing information and one complete.*

To take this further, *show them two invitations which have all the success criteria fulfilled, but where one is better than the other.* Their analysis will bring out what excellence looks like, going beyond the success criteria.

 HINTS & TIPS

1. **Don't ask the children to come up with the success criteria without using one of these strategies. It will be like pulling teeth and take ages!**

2. **Don't show them just one poor example and ask them to improve it. They need to see excellence *next to poor* to identify the elements and features of both.**

3. **Do show them two examples in which the success criteria have all been fulfilled, but they are of a different quality. You can co-construct both the criteria for the learning intention used and another, more permanent set for 'what makes the quality'.**

EVERLASTING SUCCESS CRITERIA

For every subject, you might want to display posters of co-constructed success criteria for: 'Every time we write'; 'Every time we do maths', 'Every time we use science equipment', and so on. These generic features are elements children should be aware of, whatever the context or focus learning intention, and having these posters means the criteria don't get included in every set of success criteria. A couple of examples can be seen in Figure 3.5.

Every time we write
Remember to check:
• Spelling
• Punctuation
• Handwriting
• Grammar.

Every time we do maths
Remember to:
• Make an estimate first
• Line up columns
• Check your calculations a different way
• Put the correct units in the answer (3 cm not just 3)
• Separate each calculation
• Number the different calculations.

Figure 3.5 'Every time we...' examples

TAKING IT FURTHER

MATHS PROBLEM SOLVING

These basic everlasting posters can be augmented by focusing on quality in more depth. Mathematics success criteria, for instance, are straightforward if the skill being taught has clear steps (e.g. equations, any column calculations), but need a different approach for more open maths problems. Whenever children are given 'word problems', they need problem-solving success criteria rather than definite steps. To co-construct, place a word problem under the visualiser, solved by a previous child, or made up by you, in which the problem has the following features:

• The important words have been highlighted

• An estimate has been written

• Diagrams have been used

- Working out is shown

- The answer is written with a comment about how close it was to the estimate.

Ask the children to tell their learning partner one strategy the person used in solving this problem and then gather their responses.

QUALITY IN WRITING

Often, children are told that good writing is created by using various tools such as similes, adjectives, personification, and so on. National tests in which these items are judged have sometimes resulted in children placing them in their writing, whether they enhance it or not. Of course, writing tools need to be taught, but the starting point should be the key success pointers of any good writing: the author's intent and the impact on the reader. Children can be asked, before they write, what impact they want this writing to have on the reader. This alone fires their imagination and brings their intentions to the forefront. We can also include some of the key features of good writing as a general guideline, as in the following.

WHAT MAKES GOOD WRITING?

- **What do you want your reader to think, feel and imagine? (Horror? Pity? Anger? Amusement?)**

- **What techniques will do this best?**

- **Have your adjectives told the reader something they didn't know? (Not 'wet' water or 'white' snow!)**

- **Only use writing tools if they make it better – sometimes less is more.**

- **Try improving verbs rather than simply adding lots of adjectives.**

WRITING UP LEARNING INTENTIONS AND SUCCESS CRITERIA

Although it helps to have the whole learning intention for a lesson written up at the front (after a prior knowledge discussion), it is unnecessary for children to spend time copying this into their books – a short abbreviation as a title in their books saves children hours of wasted time.

Success criteria, once co-constructed, need to be visible in the room while children are using them, on the screen, working wall or flip chart. It is unnecessary for children to copy them into their books, unless you feel this has a positive impact rather than being done for the sake of it. With closed success criteria, it could be argued that it is helpful for children to have these in their books to tick off, but with open success criteria, as in writing, ticking them off seems to imply that the work is done. Success criteria in writing do not guarantee quality, only inclusion. Quality comes from children's own reading experience being applied and the all-important class analysis of what good writing looks like. My preference is not to have the criteria written in books, although older children can create their own criteria in their own words to remember certain maths skills, for instance, once they feel they have grasped them, and have them for reference in the backs of their maths books or in a separate booklet. Teachers' professional judgement should rule, asking these two important questions: Why am I doing this? What is its impact? If the answer to either is for accountability reasons, it should be rethought. The only right answer is that you know it improves learning.

NOTE IT DOWN

DECIDE WHICH OF THE ELEMENTS OUTLINED IN THIS CHAPTER
ARE WORKING WELL IN YOUR CLASS/SCHOOL, WHICH NEED
SOME MINOR MODIFICATION AND WHICH NEED MORE CAREFUL
INVESTIGATION AND THOUGHT. REMEMBER THAT TAKING THINGS
SLOWLY AND DOING THEM WELL WILL BE MORE EFFECTIVE
THAN TRYING TO INTRODUCE TOO MUCH AT ONCE.

Element of formative assessment: sharing learning intentions (L.I.s) and co-constructing success criteria	Working well	Need to modify	Need to start (add by when)	Need to investigate/ think about
Deciding which L.I.s are knowledge and which are skills				
Providing knowledge organisers as summary references to aid retrieval				
Having closed L.I.s as 'rules' and open L.I.s as 'tools'				
Decontextualising appropriate L.I.s so that they can be transferred to different contexts				
Giving knowledge equal status by showing the key knowledge points alongside the skill success criteria				
Co-constructing via giving 2–3 examples to identify features				
Co-constructing via comparing excellent and poor examples				

Element of formative assessment: sharing learning intentions (L.I.s) and co-constructing success criteria	Working well	Need to modify	Need to start (add by when)	Need to investigate/ think about
Co-constructing via demonstrating at the visualiser				
Co-constructing via demonstrating how **not** to do it				
Co-constructing via 'Spot the mistake'				
Co-constructing via eavesdropping				
Co-constructing everlasting posters				
Having only titles in books and success criteria in the room, unless the impact is worth the time it takes to write in books				

ANSWERS TO KNOWLEDGE AND SKILLS

Where **skill** is procedural and **knowledge** is factual, the answers are as follows:

- Times table facts (knowledge)
- Writing a characterisation (skill)
- The impact of steam power (knowledge)
- Solving quadratic equations (skill)
- Using watercolours (skill)
- Properties of 2D shapes (knowledge)
- Multiplying with the column method (skill)
- Key events of the Great Fire of London (knowledge).

CHAPTER 4
IN-LESSON FEEDBACK – HOW CAN WE GIVE FEEDBACK DURING LESSONS?

This chapter explores in-the-moment feedback, with a particular focus on:

- Student-to-teacher feedback
- Questioning and probing student understanding
- On-the-move questioning and feedback
- Mid-lesson learning stops
- Peer feedback.

Feedback can be powerful but is variable in its effect. Its effectiveness depends on many factors, such as the following:

- High self-efficacy of the child to be able to receive feedback with confidence

- A good relationship between the giver, whether adult or peer, and the child so that the feedback is trusted

- Being either immediate, or in some cases, delayed

- Matching the stage of learning of the child or the topic, whether surface, deep or transfer

- Being interpreted correctly and specific enough to give support

- Whether it is acted upon and improves performance and learning.

STUDENT-TO-TEACHER FEEDBACK

'The mistake I made was seeing feedback as something teachers provided to students. I discovered that feedback is most powerful when it is from the student to the teacher.'

Hattie, 2012

Student-to-teacher feedback refers to the power of teachers seeing everything happening in the classroom as feedback about what needs to happen next. This includes children's successes, errors and misconceptions, when they are misbehaving or working hard, and when they are distracted or trying to avoid working. Instead of blaming children, we need to accept what we see in front of us as feedback, and then consider what might need to change.

As most learning happens during rather than after lessons, capitalising on the golden moment requires using strategies to uncover children's current understanding and to give them feedback while there is still time to influence what they do. The first step is to normalise and celebrate error (see Chapter 1), so that children readily share their misunderstandings or their feeling of being stuck. The culture of the classroom needs to support learning, with no competitive rewards or ability grouping, which only lead to complacency or demoralisation, creating barriers to children's self-efficacy.

Everything is feedback to the teacher – for instance, when a student is...

- **Struggling**: cognitive challenge is appropriate but if most of the class is struggling, they need more input, or to go back a step.

- **Unfocused**: are you overloading their working memory? Break it down and provide props for retrieving information which is needed for the task.

- **Unmotivated**: are there ability groups or unfair rewards which demotivate students, as the expectations of their achievement seem to have already been decided?

- **Off task**: is there task avoidance because the task is not understood or is too complex?

- **Misbehaving**: are behaviour expectations clear and/or is this a way of a student boosting their self-esteem to make up for failure even when they try their hardest?

Taking account of everything seen and heard as feedback enables teaching and learning to be synchronised and powerful.

'Feedback to teachers makes learning visible.'
Hattie, 2012

The following sections outline tried-and-tested strategies for uncovering and reacting to student understanding during lessons: questioning, on-the-move feedback, mid-lesson learning stops and cooperative peer feedback.

QUESTIONING AND PROBING STUDENT UNDERSTANDING

'The most important single factor influencing learning is what the learner already knows. Ascertain this and teach accordingly.'
Ausubel, 1968

A **prior knowledge question** at the beginning of a lesson, before the learning intention is shared, can reveal whether the planned lesson for today will be appropriate. The template questions in Table 4.1 can be used for any subject and with any age group.

Table 4.1   Template questions with examples

Question template	Example	Example	Example
Range of answers	What is 5 squared minus 3 squared? Discuss: 11, 16, 2, 13, 2 squared	What makes plants grow? Discuss: water, sand, electric light, chocolate, sunlight, milk, chips	Which strategies are likely to persuade? Discuss: evidence, bias, empathy, bullying, objectivity, bribery

Question template	Example	Example	Example
Agree or disagree?	This picture shows a Viking. Agree or disagree? Say why...	Goldilocks was a burglar. Agree or disagree? Say why...	45% of 365 is greater than 54% of 285. Agree or disagree? Say why...
Odd one out	Which of these is odd? Triangle, square, circle, rectangle, pentagon. Say why...	Which of these is odd? Slowly, carefully, bright, happily. Say why...	Which of these is odd? Nuts, meat, eggs, lettuce, fish. Say why...
What went wrong?	'The girl stared after some minutes rain fell on her head she wore a rain hat' Discuss...	(Picture of a circuit not connected properly) Discuss...	$18 \times 5 = 10 \times 5 + 9 \times 5 = 50 + 45 = 95$ Discuss....
Explain to another student...	...how you know that 3/4 is bigger than 2/3.	...the difference between an adjective and an adverb.	...how photosynthesis happens.
Opposites	Why is this meal healthy and this one not?	Why is this calculation right $(8 \div 0.5 = 16)$ and this one wrong $(8 \times 0.5 = 16)$?	Why does this toy move and this one not?

USING THE TEMPLATES

HOW TO USE THE TEMPLATES: FOR LESSON STARTS

- Look at the learning intention for the lesson and choose the best template to write up. Think about what you need to establish before you proceed with the lesson – you are finding out what they already know or have remembered. The question could be focused around:

- ○ what they already know before you start any teaching of the content or

- ○ what they have remembered from yesterday's/last week's lesson since you started teaching it or

- ○ an assessment of what they have learned by the end of a unit of work. Any time is useful!

- Tell students to discuss the question with their talk partner for about 3 minutes, while you walk around the classroom, listening to their conversations (see Chapter 2 on talk partners).

- Decide whether you need to continue with a recap of yesterday's learning, a reteaching of yesterday's learning, or to skip your plans and move on to more challenging content. Some teachers say that the starter question sometimes becomes the focus of the entire lesson!

HOW TO USE THE TEMPLATES: AT ANY TIME DURING A LESSON

- Present one of the questions, or a multiple-choice test question, to check current understanding, giving a short time for either paired discussion or silent thinking. Then for an open-ended question, take a few comments randomly. Or, for a multiple-choice question, either (a) ask for the possible answers (e.g. a, b, c) to be written on whiteboards and held up for you to see; or (b) ask for one, two or three fingers to be held up to indicate their preferred answer.

- Have a 'sentence stems' poster to assist students' responses, when you want the discussion to be opened up (see Figure 4.1).

CHECKING UNDERSTANDING AT THE END OF LESSONS

TEXT MESSAGE

Students could write you a text message on a mobile phone paper template if there is something they want to tell or ask you, but didn't get the chance to in the lesson (e.g. a student might write, *Could you start with lower numbers and work our way up to bigger numbers, please?*).

Sentence-stem examples	
I agree because…	
	But what if…?
I disagree because…	
	Can you say more about…?
I need more information about…	
	I think…
I like that because…	
	I'm not sure because…
Would it be the same if…?	
	It depends on…

Figure 4.1   'What you might say' sentence-stem examples

MINI QUESTIONNAIRE

Given a list of techniques you used to help them learn this learning intention, ask students to tick which strategies helped them the most and what would have helped them more (e.g. *Which of these things helped you learn long multiplication? What else could I have done to help you learn it?*).

EXIT CARD

- Ask children to do one more maths question, for instance, and to hand it to you as they leave the classroom (see Figure 4.2).

What is a factor?	I can do this ☐
	I need more input ☐
Show the factor pairs of 24:	Comment: _____ _____ _____

Figure 4.2 An 'exit card' maths question

- Give them a sheet with two columns labelled 'My wonderful mistake' and 'What I learnt', if the lesson involved estimating or trial and error.

ON-THE-MOVE QUESTIONING AND FEEDBACK

Kluger and DeNisi's (1996) research review showed that feedback only leads to learning gains *when it includes guidance about how to improve*.

'The greatest motivational benefits will come from focusing feedback on:
The qualities of the students' work, and not on comparison with other students;
Specific ways in which the student's work could be improved.'
Crooks, 2001: 13–15

The word 'specific' in Crook's research is significant: it is often the case that, instead of giving specific, concrete strategies to help students move from what they have achieved to what we want them to achieve, teachers instead simply reiterate the desired goal – a reminder prompt. For example, *You need to improve these two long sentences*, merely reiterates the learning goal of 'To be able to write effective long sentences'. Better advice would be, for instance, *Improve these two long sentences, using some short noun phrases, such as old features, thin lips, grating voice*, or similar. Giving 'for instances' and specific advice is key to the quality of an improvement suggestion.

HELICOPTERING AND LANDING

Make it the norm to be constantly on the move around the classroom, pen in hand, while the children are involved in their independent or partner work. This enables you to catch slips, misconceptions, children who are stuck or muddled, or those who haven't yet started or have misunderstood the task. Try walking around in the first 5 minutes of the independent work, to check that every child is on track and knows what to do, before you start interacting with individuals.

While on the move, you might simply put a dot in the margin of a child's writing and say 'Look for a spelling error in this line', or 'I think there's an error in this calculation – check it before you carry on.' With writing, you might say 'Great description of the sea here – your simile is very vivid. Could you add more detail using your other senses?' or 'Read the first sentence to me. You paused there and it sounded good. Does it need some punctuation?'

You might decide to pair two children up for a short time, so that one can share his or her learning with the other or explain something misunderstood; you might also want to take a few children to a table to talk to them together. Obviously, if your helicoptering reveals that most of the children are struggling negatively, you probably need to stop the whole class and go over the learning in a different way, or ask a child to come up and explain to the class.

Whether you spend a few seconds or a few minutes with the children, by the time the independent time has ended you will have written in many children's books and, more importantly, provided verbal feedback which the children have been able to act upon there and then. Feedback after lessons is often too late to have any impact.

ON-THE-MOVE FEEDBACK: THINGS YOU MIGHT ASK

- Tell me what you're going to do first/next.

- What do you mean by…? (A key question, even if the teacher thinks s/he knows what they mean by it)

- Why do you think…?

- Give me an example of what you mean. (Another key question that often reveals misconceptions)

- Can you develop that? Tell me more…

- So why is this one better than that? (A key question as a concrete example is available)

- How could you change this to make it clearer?

- Interrupt me if I've misunderstood your question or your work….

- What do you need more of: practice, effort, time or input?

 HINTS & TIPS

1. Have your pen ready to write straight into the children's books if necessary.

2. Get down to the child's level and speak as quietly as you can to avoid disturbing the other children.

3. Make sure the success criteria are visible during the lesson, and encourage students to check these from time to time. See Chapter 2 for further detail on success criteria, but the key reminder while children are working would be whether they are rules (compulsory success criteria for closed learning intentions) or tools (a set of suggested strategies for open learning intentions).

4. Point out successes first, before suggesting any improvements.

5. Don't write VF (verbal feedback) on children's work every time you speak to them – that is your job and it doesn't need proof that you did it!

6. Go for one improvement to be done at a time.

7. Don't interrupt a talk partner or group discussion by asking a question if they are on track. The moment will be lost...

GETTING THE TIMING RIGHT

Delay feedback for higher achievers to encourage them to check their work independently and self-regulate. You'll also want to delay feedback when students are 'in the pit', encountering necessary, desirable difficulties, intervening only if necessary.

MATCHING FEEDBACK TO THE STAGE OF LEARNING

Learning is first at the **cognitive, 'surface' stage**, when feedback needs to focus around identifying and naming, using success criteria, following methods and structure (e.g. identifying different fractions).

It then moves on to the **associative, 'deep' stage**, when feedback encourages relationships between ideas, causes and effects, and more expert understanding (e.g. knowing equivalent fractions and how they relate to one another).

Students finally reach the **automatic, 'transfer' stage**, which is when concepts are stored in long-term memory. Feedback at this stage needs to focus on applying that knowledge to other contexts. It is also the stage when self-regulation is most developed; students self-assess, check their work and make decisions about possible improvements, encouraged by you and each other (e.g. being able to find fractions of any quantity in any context and use them for any operation).

MID-LESSON LEARNING STOPS

Mid-lesson learning stops give feedback to all children at once. The suggested routine is as follows:

- Let them know, in advance, that you will be randomly choosing one child's work to be placed under the visualiser to celebrate their successes and offer advice for improvement.

- Ask the class, in pairs, to discuss the projected work for a short time to decide which bits are most successful and why. Take some of the responses and emphasise the reasons for the success.

- Pairs then identify anything that could be improved and offer *specific examples* rather than general comments (e.g. *How about saying the clouds looked down on the scene below?* or *You needed to include centimetres in your answer.*).

- Ask the author of the work to choose among the given suggestions or to come up with their own idea. The author gets the final say.

- After this whole-class analysis, ask the class to review their own work, making any improvements of their own in a different-coloured pen.

The benefits of a mid-lesson learning stop are the following:

- A mid-lesson learning stop models the process of identifying success and improvement so that children are trained to do this alone, emphasising the value of continual review of one's learning.

- It confirms, mid-lesson, whether students feel they are on track.

- It gives students examples of excellence and ideas to inspire their own work.

- It resonates with all students who might have similar mistakes or improvement needs.

 HINTS & TIPS

1. Mid-lesson learning stops build on a healthy learning culture with high self-efficacy, in which children are excited by challenge and mistakes and know they can trust the teacher and the other children to support their learning.

2. Teachers often start this strategy by using anonymous pieces of work from a different class, so that children get used to the process and realise that everyone is treated the same, regardless of their achievement level.

3. Reassure children that you know they are not finished and are only half way through.

4. Make sure, no matter how limited a random piece of work might be, that you always start with the successes: 'What do we really like and why?' before moving on to the improvement suggestions.

5. Pre-empt children suggesting improvements which are not related to the learning intention, such as

(Continued)

> handwriting, and focus them on the success criteria.
> If it is a piece of writing, ask which are the best bits, the
> answers often superseding the success criteria.

6.   Once the routine is established, children will be excited
     about having their work analysed.

PEER FEEDBACK

Children in pairs, activated as learning resources for each other, are powerful feedback givers and receivers, using child language which is often more clearly understood than the words of a teacher. Students have more natural conversations when working with their peers than when speaking with a teacher. They are more likely, for instance, to interrupt each other or ask for clarification.

Using the random talk partner system described in Chapter 2, children experience a range of both social and cognitive pairings: one week as the higher achiever in a pair, explaining and consolidating; the next week maybe learning from a higher achiever. Children often say that even a partner who struggles with writing often has good ideas. Two children sitting together doing different levels of mathematics often learn from each other, both revisiting or augmenting existing knowledge.

During the course of a lesson, and during the independent time, learning partners have many opportunities for discussion about the learning. One particularly effective strategy is cooperative feedback discussions, when children have completed their first drafts of any writing assignments.

COOPERATIVE FEEDBACK DISCUSSIONS

In the past, the general interpretation of peer-marking or peer assessment has been the swapping of students' work. The student becomes a teacher, working on their own, making comments on the work about what they liked and what could be improved. Having seen many examples of pieces of work given comments by students in this way, the general impression has been that their comments tend to be superficial and relatively unhelpful. *Cooperative feedback*, in which the author has the last word and makes the improvements as a result of discussions with a learning partner, however, is an entirely different and more productive experience, a testament to the power of structured collaboration. Training students in this involves the following steps:

1. Both students read and discuss one of their pieces together, with one book on top of the other to avoid being distracted by their own work. The student whose work it is has control of the pen and ultimate decision making.

2. Together, through discussion, they decide the best bits, which they might disagree about, but reasons are given and those bits underlined.

3. They then talk about improvements that could be made and the author makes them on the piece, there and then, writing the improvement, often in a different colour. As the available space for improvements will be limited, many schools leave the left-hand side of students' books blank, so that improvements can be written with no limits and retain legibility. No comments are written on the piece by either student, because this would take away precious time when the actual improvements could be made. Again, the author has the last word on the choice of improvement.

4. The children then go through the same process with their partner's work.

5. With older students and more complex work, they might then separate and attend to their improvements alone after the cooperative discussion.

Observations and video evidence of this process have revealed that:

- When the author reads their work out loud, pen in hand, they see their errors immediately. In the case of mathematics, the equivalent would be to talk through their steps and their thinking, in line with the success criteria, with their partner.

- Students have more natural conversations, interrupting each other or asking for clarification and so on, than when they are in dialogue with a teacher.

HINTS & TIPS

1. Becoming teachers for each other is a complex business so needs modelling and coaching. We need to make clear to students that their partner is only there to give them ideas, not to dictate, and this should be modelled (e.g. *Thank you – that's made me think of another idea.*).

2. The cooperative improvement process can be used across all subjects. Instead of one 'book' sitting on top of the other, they might have one piece of maths work, one piece of artwork, one technology model, and so on, between them, so that they are not distracted, mid-conversation, to look at their own work.

3. This three-step practice of mid-lesson stops followed by self-review then cooperative feedback discussions, leads to students working much harder than they used to, compared to mainly uninterrupted work during lessons, with books handed in for copious marking by the teacher, given back at a later time when the feedback is too late to do anything about, and is limited to written comments only. Of course, there are times when students should not be interrupted in their thinking, but when we are skill building, constant review is more helpful than waiting till the product is finished and then needing to go back and redo it.

4. Mid-lesson stops followed by self-review then cooperative feedback discussions lead to students working much harder than they used to. As Jackson (2009) said: 'Feedback should be more work for the recipient than the donor.'

5. When we are skill building, constant review and feedback are more helpful than post-lesson written comments, which require waiting until the product is finished then asking students to go back and redo the work.

NOTE IT DOWN

DECIDE WHICH OF THE ELEMENTS OUTLINED IN THIS CHAPTER ARE WORKING WELL IN YOUR CLASS/SCHOOL, WHICH NEED SOME MINOR MODIFICATION AND WHICH NEED MORE CAREFUL INVESTIGATION AND THOUGHT. REMEMBER THAT TAKING THINGS SLOWLY AND DOING THEM WELL WILL BE MORE EFFECTIVE THAN TRYING TO INTRODUCE TOO MUCH AT ONCE.

Element of formative assessment: in-lesson feedback	Working well	Need to modify	Need to start (add by when)	Need to investigate/ think about
Consciously seeing everything as feedback for me				
Using prior knowledge templates at lesson starts to inform what follows				
Using hinge questions mid-lesson to check on current understanding				
Introducing sentence stems to aid class discussion				

(Continued)

Element of formative assessment: in-lesson feedback	Working well	Need to modify	Need to start (add by when)	Need to investigate/ think about
Introducing a text message or exit cards				
Asking for children's opinions about what helped them learn a particular unit best and what would have helped them further				
On the move, pen in hand, during independent work, stopping to question and give feedback in the moment				
Introducing mid-lesson learning stops in which one child's work is analysed for success and improvements				
Introducing cooperative paired improvement after first drafts of any work				

CHAPTER 5
POST-LESSON FEEDBACK AND MARKING – HOW TO MAKE THEM MANAGEABLE?

This chapter looks at post-lesson feedback, with a focus on written feedback and strategies. Topics covered are:

- Grading
- Whole-class feedback
- Feedback to and from parents.

Teachers have, for many decades, often spent much of their post-lesson time on marking books – giving written feedback to children mainly for accountability purposes, sometimes even believing that the more marking is done, the better you are as a teacher. Over the last few years, with a greater emphasis on questioning whether what we do in school has an impact on learning, schools have been rethinking the best use of their time for the greatest impact on learning, while preserving a realistic and healthy work–life balance.

There is only so much time once the school day has finished and, if there is to be a balance between work and personal life, some decisions have to be made. 'In the moment' feedback has more impact on learning than written feedback after the lesson, hence the focus of the previous chapter. The number of words said face to face to a child in a 2-minute conversation during the independent stage of a lesson, would take up several pages of written comments in the child's book, and has the advantage of a one-to-one relationship enhancement. Added to this, the child can now act on the feedback immediately, making any changes to their learning while they are still in the context of that learning. Getting a written comment after the lesson is harder for the child to read, interpret and act upon once the context and time have passed, but might be useful if used occasionally and children's improvements may be followed up via class discussion and visualiser use.

> *'The most effective feedback is just feedback that our students actually use in improving their learning.'*
> *Wiliam and Leahy, 2015: 107*

GRADING

Grading is mainly carried out in secondary schools, but has negative impact on student motivation, especially if given before the learning is over for a particular unit of study. When a grade is assigned, students care about how they have done compared to others, thus receiving ego-related feedback, which damages learning. Like ability grouping, grading leads to students being defined by their grade ('I'm an A student'). Studies show that grading decreases student achievement, leading to complacency for higher achievers and demoralisation for lower achievers.

SUMMATIVE GRADING

When grading is summative (i.e. at the end of a topic or programme), it can and does provide a judgement of the alignment of the student's work to the expected standard. As Alfie Kohn (1994) said, 'Never grade students while they are still learning'.

> 'Teachers should be aware of the impact that comments, marks and grades can have on learners' confidence and enthusiasm and should be as constructive as possible in the feedback that they give.'
> Assessment Reform Group, 2002

 CASE STUDY

Ruth Butler (1988) carried out a controlled experimental study in which she set up three ways of giving feedback to three different groups of same-age/ability students:

1. **Marks or grade**

2. **Comments**

3. **Marks or grades and comments.**

(Continued)

The study showed that learning gains (measured by exam results) were greater for the comment only group, with the other two groups showing no gains. Where even positive comments accompanied grades, interviews with students of low grades revealed that they believed the teacher was 'being kind' and that the grade was the real indicator of the quality of their work.

WRITTEN FEEDBACK

It is important that children know that we have looked at their work, but the decision to write improvement comments on every child's piece of work must be worth the time it takes, so it is a matter of teacher judgement and to be weighed up against the time needed for planning lessons and sourcing examples of excellence, for instance.

The most powerful feedback, as emphasised in the previous chapter, is the in-the-moment feedback, verbal or written, which teachers engage in throughout a lesson. When there have been mid-lesson learning stops, in which all are given feedback via the analysis of a random piece of work in progress, where students have self- and peer-improved and edited their work, a further written improvement suggestion by the teacher seems tokenistic.

ACKNOWLEDGEMENT MARKING AND CHECKING BOOKS

This is where a brief comment ('Really liked your improvement, Alfie') or even a signature, shows the child that you have read their work and is most suitable when a great deal of feedback has taken place within the lesson. Books marked in this way are then checked for planning purposes, maybe piling up the books ready for the next lesson.

SUCCESS AND IMPROVEMENT COMMENTS

In the past, the term 'next steps' has led teachers to write comments advising students 'Next time, remember to...', which can also be a waste of time, as the advice might not be remembered at a later date, in a different context, especially for primary-aged students. For secondary students, advice about future work can be informative, although the process of making improvements on existing work enables the student to rethink, refine and possibly redraft, so that this process becomes a natural habit. The advent of many schools highlighting three successes and one improvement in different colours on a child's work, was an attempt to reduce the marking workload, so that a child could see instantly what was successful and what needed to be improved. If you believe an improvement comment – to be acted upon by the child at the next lesson – is worth the time it takes, the levels of improvement prompts for writing, given in Table 5.1, could be useful, as they provide specific guidance rather than comments which are too general to be helpful.

Table 5.1   Levels of improvement prompts for writing

L.I. Descriptive setting	
Context: The Sea	
Reminder prompt (higher achievers in writing)	Remember to use your senses:
Scaffolded prompt (middle achievers in writing)	Describe the way the waves sounded using personification perhaps...
	Were the waves calm and gentle? Was the sound crashing and thunderous?
	Use a simile: The sound of the waves reminded her of...
Example prompt (lower achievers in writing)	**Choose one of these, or make up your own:**
	The sea was blue-green, fiercely crashing and raging.
	The waves, white-tipped, ebbed and flowed, receding into the distance.

HINTS & TIPS

1.   **Specific improvement prompts can be used verbally for on-the-move feedback or in written form after the lesson.**

(Continued)

2. Remember to start every feedback exchange with an identification of successes.

3. Improvement suggestions can be anything from adding new words or phrases, changing something, such as punctuation, extending or reshaping. In mathematics, it might be checking the success criteria and redoing them with advice along the same lines.

4. Children will need dedicated time at the beginning of the next lesson to read and then make their improvement.

5. If the left-hand side of exercise books is always left blank, this provides a perfect space for later improvements to be made, alongside their original attempts. Having that space leads to children having more scope for their improvements.

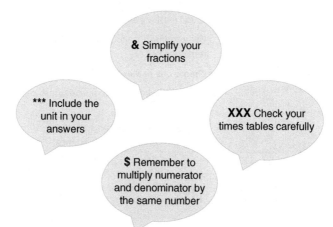

Figure 5.1 Examples of symbols for common maths mistakes

CODED MARKING

Apart from highlighting success and improvements, time can be saved by using either symbols or codes, as long as you know that these have a positive impact on children's learning. For maths, **symbols for common mistakes** can be used as the only marks written on children's work (see some examples in Figure 5.1). At the beginning of the next lesson, children can then see an explanation of each symbol and spend some time correcting one or two examples.

Numbers or letters can also be used, if children have copies of target sheets or access to posters on working walls (see Table 5.2).

Table 5.2   An example of a target sheet

A	Write in clear sentences.
B	Use commas to separate parts of a sentence and for lists.
C	Use punctuation marks correctly (? ! ").
D	Make sure commonly used words are spelt correctly.
E	Use connectives to link sentences together.
F	Use paragraphs to separate ideas.
G	Make your writing suitable for the audience – e.g. formal/ informal.

WHOLE-CLASS FEEDBACK

If you find that whole-class feedback will have the best impact, there are several strategies you can try:

- The teacher reads through the books, taking notes as s/he goes, then passes the information to the children at the next lesson, usually consisting of information about their general response to the task (e.g. 'Most of you were able to show … Some of you went further, like this example ... You all need to work on ... You all need more input and revision on ... Here's what I think we need to do next...').

- The teacher completes a more formal, whole-class feedback sheet, using their own headings, which is projected and discussed with the class at the next lesson.

- The teacher does the above but makes copies of the whole-class feedback sheet and gives it out so that all children have a copy for future reference. This is clearly the best solution, as it helps ease the cognitive load and provides children with revision material.

 HINTS & TIPS

1. Beware of over-formalised whole-class feedback forms. We are very good at systematising things which then create a greater workload. It would be better to write notes in order to feed back to the whole class, than to fill out a form which takes as much time as marking books individually.

2. Use professional judgement about which form of feedback will work best: in-lesson feedback most of the time, with acknowledgement marking, marking codes, improvement prompts, to be acted upon as needed and when it will have enough impact to warrant the time spent on it.

3. When feedback and marking policy decisions are being made, two key questions should be asked each time:

    - Why are we doing it?

    - What is its impact?

If the answer to either is anything other than improving children's learning, the policy should be rejected.

FEEDBACK TO AND FROM PARENTS

WHAT MATTERS MOST

Hong and Ho (2005) found that parent aspirations were the most important influence on their children's achievement, whereas parental supervision, in the forms of monitoring students' homework, time watching screens and time going out with friends, appeared to have a negative effect on the educational aspirations of adolescent students. Also having a negative effect were external rewards, negative control and restrictions, as a result of unsatisfactory grades.

To augment these findings, schools need to work in partnership with parents and other caregivers to make their expectations appropriately challenging and clear.

'Parents should be educated in the language of schooling so that the home and school can share in the expectations, and the child does not have to live in two worlds – with little understanding between the two.'
Hattie, 2009

FEEDBACK TO PARENTS

Many teachers share children's learning via apps such as 'Seesaw', and some schools now include learning dispositions in reports alongside traditional reports on academic learning.

Sheringham Primary School in Newham uses an interesting format to inform parents about children's learning dispositions, listing resilience, independence, cooperation, and so on. The first two learning powers are shown in Figure 5.2, an example of one child's report.

In Year 6, how is my child learning?		
Resilience	Is persistent and doesn't give up when faced with things that are difficult. Tries different approaches to find what works.	☐☐☐☐☒☐☐☐ ☹ ☺
Independence	Can work well alone, focusing on the task and ignoring disruptions. Is self-confident and can make their own decisions.	☐☐☐☐☐☒☐☐ ☹ ☺

Figure 5.2 Example of showing learning dispositions in a child's report

Source: Sheringham Primary School, Newham

CHILD-LED PARENT CONFERENCES

Hawthornden School in Mid-Lothian decided to provide open afternoons built into the school calendar for what it called 'PATPAL' (students as teachers/parents as learners in which children taught their parents something they were learning in their classroom), thus providing perhaps a more informal way of parents being able to see not just what, but also how their child is learning.

Merlyn School in Wales introduced learner-led conferences instead of parent open evenings, in which children present their learning and talk about where they are, how they are progressing and their next steps. This has had a positive impact on conversations parents have with teachers about learning.

FEEDBACK FROM PARENTS

Apart from day-to-day arrangements for parents to speak to school staff, most schools have parent questionnaires which provide data about parent satisfaction with the school and their child's progress. Holding parent evenings, in which school policy is explained and questions can be asked, is also a common practice.

One school introduced a parent 'graffiti board' for feedback and feedforward, and the children are encouraged to take their parents to write things on the board. Taking the topic of homework, comments revealed that the parents of younger children liked project work and getting involved, but, as the children got older, parental enthusiasm waned. As a consequence, the staff has reviewed the school's homework policy.

NOTE IT DOWN

DECIDE WHICH OF THE ELEMENTS OUTLINED IN THIS CHAPTER ARE WORKING WELL IN YOUR CLASS/SCHOOL, WHICH NEED SOME MINOR MODIFICATION AND WHICH NEED MORE CAREFUL INVESTIGATION AND THOUGHT. REMEMBER THAT TAKING THINGS SLOWLY AND DOING THEM WELL WILL BE MORE EFFECTIVE THAN TRYING TO INTRODUCE TOO MUCH AT ONCE.

Element of formative assessment: post-lesson feedback	Working well	Need to modify	Need to start (add by when)	Need to investigate/ think about
Keeping a record of students' grades but only giving them a grade at the end of a unit of work				
Giving feedback for each assignment which gives comments on success and how to improve				
Giving acknowledgement marking (signature or tick) to show the work has been looked at when oral or whole-class feedback is given				
Giving whole-class feedback alongside acknowledgement marking				

Element of formative assessment: post-lesson feedback	Working well	Need to modify	Need to start (add by when)	Need to investigate/ think about
Getting post-lesson feedback from students				
Introducing coded marking where appropriate				
Asking for their opinions about what helped them learn a particular unit best and what would have helped them further				
Allowing time at beginnings of lessons, for students to make one improvement to their work based on the improvement feedback				
Getting feedback from parents about specific issues (e.g. homework)				
Giving parents feedback about the student's achievement in metacognition aspects (e.g. resilience, perseverance)				

USEFUL ONLINE RESOURCES

Assessment Reform Group (2002) Assessment for Learning: Ten Principles. Available at: www.assessment-reform-group.org.uk

Numbered targets can be found at http://learningfrommymistakesenglish. blogspot.com

See teachers in action co-constructing success criteria on the video platform, at www.shirleyclarke-education.org

Christopher Curtis (2016) Twitter @Xris32

Craft sticks or lolly sticks are available from online retailers, e.g. amazon. co.uk, hobbycraft.co.uk, theworks.co.uk

REFERENCES

Assessment Reform Group (2002) Assessment for Learning: Ten Principles (www.assessment-reform-group.org.uk).

Ausubel, D.P. (1968) *Educational Psychology: A Cognitive View*. New York: Holt, Rinehart & Winston.

Baines, E., Blatchford, P. and Kutnick, P. (2017) *Promoting Effective Group Work in the Primary Classroom*. Oxon: Routledge.

Butler, R. (1988) 'Enhancing and undermining intrinsic motivation: The effects of task-involving and ego-involving evaluation on interest and performance', *British Journal of Educational Psychology*, 58(1): 1–14.

Clarke, S. and Muncaster, K. (2019) *Thinking Classrooms*. London: Rising Stars.

Claxton, G. (2018) *The Learning Power Approach*. Carmarthen: Crown House.

Cook, S.B., Scruggs, T.E., Mastropieri, M.A. and Casto, G.C. (1985) 'Handicapped students as tutors', *Journal of Special Education*, 19(4): 483–92.

Crooks, T. (2001) 'The validity of formative assessments', *British Educational Research Association Annual Conference*. University of Leeds, September, pp. 13–15.

Education Endowment Fund (EEF) (2018) Metacognition and Self-regulation (https://educationendowmentfoundation.org.uk/evidence-summaries/teaching-learning-toolkit/meta-cognition-and-self-regulation).

Hattie, J. (2009) *Visible Learning*. London: Routledge.

Hattie, J. (2012) *Visible Learning for Teachers*. London: Routledge.

Hattie, J. and Clarke, S. (2019) *Visible Learning Feedback*. London: Routledge.

Hattie, J.A.C. and Donoghue, G.M. (2016) 'Learning strategies: A synthesis and conceptual model', *npj Science of Learning*, 1: 16013 (www.nature.com/articles/npjscilearn201613).

Hong, S. and Ho, H.-Z. (2005) 'Direct and indirect longitudinal effects of parental involvement on student achievement: Second-order latent growth modelling across ethnic groups', *Journal of Educational Psychology*, 97(1): 32–42.

Jackson, R.R. (2009) *Never Work Harder than Your Students, and Other Principles of Great Teaching*. Alexandria, VA: ASCD.

Kluger, A.N. and DeNisi, A. (1996) 'The effects of feedback interventions on performance: A historical review, a meta-analysis, and a preliminary feedback intervention theory', *Psychological Bulletin*, 119(2): 254–84.

Kohn, A. (1994) 'Grading: The issue is not how but why', *Educational Leadership*, 52(2): 38–41.

Lepper, M.R. and Hodell, M. (1989) 'Intrinsic motivation in the classroom', in C. Ames and R. Ames (eds), *Research on Motivation in the Classroom* (Vol. 3, pp. 73–105). San Diego, CA: Academic Press.

Meyer, W.-U., Mittag, W. and Engler, U. (1986) 'Some effects of praise and blame on perceived ability and affect', *Social Cognition*, 4(3): 293–308.

Organisation for Economic Co-operation and Development (OECD) (2010) *PISA 2009 Results: What makes a school successful? Resources, policies and practices* (Vol. 4). Paris: OECD.

Sadler, R. (1989) 'Formative assessment and the design of instructional systems', *Instructional Science*, 18: 119–44.

Siciliano, J.I. (1999) 'How to incorporate cooperative learning principles in the classroom: It's more than just putting students in teams', *Journal of Management Education*, 25(1): 8–20.

Wiliam, D. and Leahy, S. (2015) *Embedding Formative Assessment: Practical Techniques for K-12 Classrooms*. West Palm Beach, FL: Learning Sciences International.

Willingham, D.T. (2009) *Why Don't Children Like School? A cognitive scientist answers questions about how the mind works and what it means for your classroom*. San Francisco, CA: Jossey-Bass.

INDEX